AlphaBasiCs

Colonial Times

from A to Z

A Bobbie Kalman Book

 Crabtree Publishing Company

www.crabtreebooks.com

AlphaBasiCs

Created by Bobbie Kalman

For Alan Laming and Patricia Guilloton,
with lots of love

Editor-in-Chief
Bobbie Kalman

Managing editor
Lynda Hale

Editors
Niki Walker
Greg Nickles

Computer design
Lynda Hale
Robert MacGregor (cover concept)

Photo research
Hannelore Sotzek

Production coordinator
Hannelore Sotzek

Separations and film
Dot 'n Line Image Inc.
CCS Princeton (cover)

Printer
Worzalla Publishing Company

Special thanks to
Cathy Grosfils, Emma L. Powers, and
the Colonial Williamsburg Foundation

Photographs and reproductions
Bridgeman/Art Resource, NY: title page (detail)
Colonial Williamsburg Foundation: pages 5, 6,
    9 (top left), 12, 16, 27, 28, 30
Samantha Crabtree: page 15
Giraudon/Art Resource, NY: page 7 (detail)
Bobbie Kalman: page 9 (top right), 10, 21
National Museum of American Art, Washington DC/
    Art Resource, NY: page 8

Illustrations
Barbara Bedell: cover and pages 4, 9, 11, 13, 14, 17,
    18, 19, 20, 21, 22-26, 31
Antoinette "Cookie" Bortolon: pages 5, 6, 10, 16, 29

Crabtree Publishing Company
www.crabtreebooks.com   1-800-387-7650

Cataloging in Publication Data
Kalman, Bobbie
    Colonial Times from A to Z

(AlphaBasiCs series)
Includes index.
ISBN 0-86505-377-4 (library bound) ISBN 0-86505-407-X (pbk.)
This alphabet book introduces aspects of life in the United States during the colonial period
(1607-1776). Topics include games, clothing, and special occasions. Tradespeople, family,
and other aspects of community life are explained.

1. United States—Social life and customs—To 1775—Juvenile literature. 2. English
language—Alphabet—Juvenile literature I. Title. II. Series: Kalman, Bobbie. AlphaBasiCs.

E162.K1995 1997   j973.2   LC 97-28800
                                                    CIP

**Published in
the United States**
PMB16A
350 Fifth Ave.
Suite 3308
New York, NY
10118

**Published
in Canada**
616 Welland Ave.
St. Catharines, Ontario
Canada
L2M 5V6

**Published in the
United Kingdom**
White Cross Mills
High Town, Lancaster
LA1 4XS
United Kingdom

**Published
in Australia**
386 Mt. Alexander Rd.
Ascot Vale (Melbourne)
VIC 3032

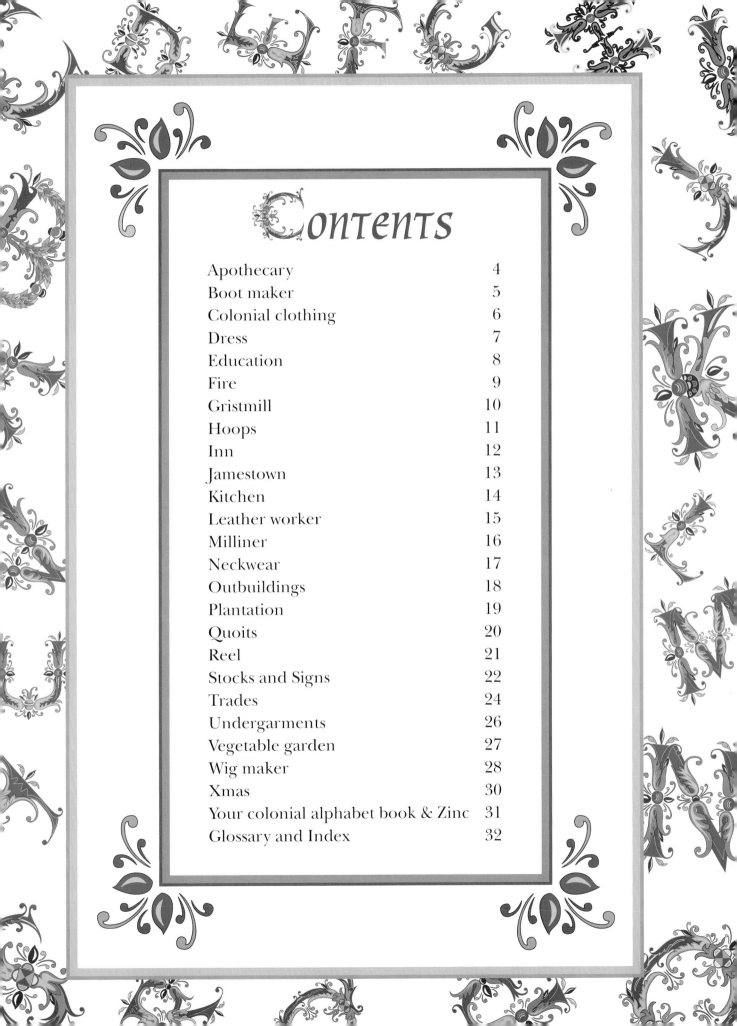

Contents

Apothecary	4
Boot maker	5
Colonial clothing	6
Dress	7
Education	8
Fire	9
Gristmill	10
Hoops	11
Inn	12
Jamestown	13
Kitchen	14
Leather worker	15
Milliner	16
Neckwear	17
Outbuildings	18
Plantation	19
Quoits	20
Reel	21
Stocks and Signs	22
Trades	24
Undergarments	26
Vegetable garden	27
Wig maker	28
Xmas	30
Your colonial alphabet book & Zinc	31
Glossary and Index	32

is for **apothecary**. In colonial times, people went to an apothecary when they were sick. Some apothecaries owned shops where they made medicines. A few apothecaries were doctors who had gone to medical school, but most learned their skills by working as **apprentices**.

An apprentice cleaned the apothecary shop and ran errands. He put dressings on wounds and learned how to make medicines from plants and other natural things. The apprentice worked for the apothecary for up to seven years before he, too, became an apothecary.

 is for **boot maker**. A boot maker made boots and shoes from leather. He could make as many as ten pairs a week. First he carved **lasts**. A last was a piece of wood that was shaped like a foot. Leather was stretched around the last, and then the sole of the boot or shoe was stitched to the leather.

There were no left or right shoes. It was easier for the boot maker to use one last as a model, so both shoes in a pair looked the same. Colonial shoes did not have laces. Many were fastened with buckles.

Some boot makers owned their own shop. They were very busy because people needed boots to ride horses. Boots also kept mud off people's feet and legs.

5

is for **colonial clothing**. Men and boys wore shirts, breeches, and waistcoats every day. In cold weather, they also wore **capes** or coats. Clothes were made from wool, silk, **linen**, and velvet. Pants and coats did not have zippers. They fastened in front with a row of buttons.

Tricornes were very popular hats. They had three corners.

Waistcoats were like vests. They were worn over a shirt and under a suit coat.

Breeches were short pants that ended just below the knees. Men did not wear long pants until the 1800s.

Stockings reached past the knees and were worn with breeches.

is for **dress**. Girls and women wore dresses, which were called **robes** or **gowns**. Most had two dresses. They wore one weekdays and saved the other for Sunday. The top of a dress was called the **bodice**. An underpetticoat, petticoat, and overskirt made up the bottom. (See page 26.)

is for **education**. There were few schools in colonial days. When there was a school, there was only one teacher for all the students. Parents paid to have their children educated. Only boys attended high school or college. At home, girls were taught to cook and sew.

*Some boys were sent away to **boarding school** because not every town had a high school. A few went to university in England or to one of the colleges in North America.*

F is for **fire**. There was no electricity in colonial days. The fireplace was used to cook meals, heat the home, and provide light for reading and sewing. Fire was necessary, but it was also dangerous. Sparks flew up the chimney and sometimes set it or the roof on fire.

(far left) People needed a lot of wood to keep a fire going. Children helped chop and fetch firewood.

*A **fire ladder** led to the roof. It allowed people to put out a chimney or roof fire quickly.*

*There were no fire hydrants or hoses. When a house was on fire, people formed a **bucket brigade**. They passed along buckets of water from a well to the burning house.*

 is for **gristmill**. A gristmill ground **grains** such as wheat and rye into flour. It also ground corn into cornmeal. This gristmill is a windmill. It uses the wind for power. Wind blows and turns the **sails** of the windmill. The sails turn **gears** inside the mill, and the gears turn a huge **grindstone**.

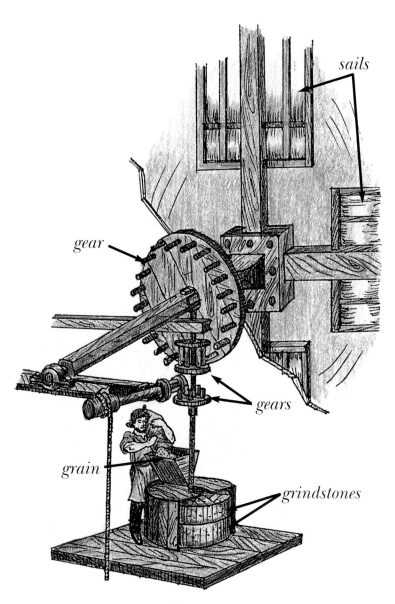

sails

gear

gears

grain

grindstones

*As the top grindstone turns, the **miller** pours corn into a hole. The corn is ground between the two stones.*

*Some towns had a wind-powered gristmill such as the one above. Others had a mill that was powered by a **water wheel**.*

 is for **hoops**. Hoops were used to make barrels and wagon wheels. When the hoops wore out, they became children's toys. A child ran beside a rolling hoop and pushed it with a stick to keep it going. Women wore a different type of hoop under their skirt to give it shape.

Hoop races were fun. Children raced their hoops along a road, across a field, or down a hill. Hoops were made of metal or wood.

*Fancy women's dresses were very wide at the hips. **Pocket hoops** gave skirts this fashionable shape.*

is for **inn**. An inn was like a small hotel. Up to six men slept in one room. Sometimes they had to share a bed with a stranger! Often, the sheets were dirty and bugs lived in the beds. Women travelers did not sleep at inns. They slept at the home of a family in town.

*People traveled from place to place by **stagecoach**. The stagecoach stopped at the inn, where travelers could get a meal as well as a place to sleep. Inns were also called **taverns**. People who lived in town often went to the tavern for a meal and some drinks.*

is for **Jamestown**. Almost 400 years ago, a group of men sailed to North America from England. They built a strong fort, shown below, and called it James Fort. Soon other people came, and Jamestown grew around the fort. It became the first capital of England's **colonies** in America.

JAMES FORT

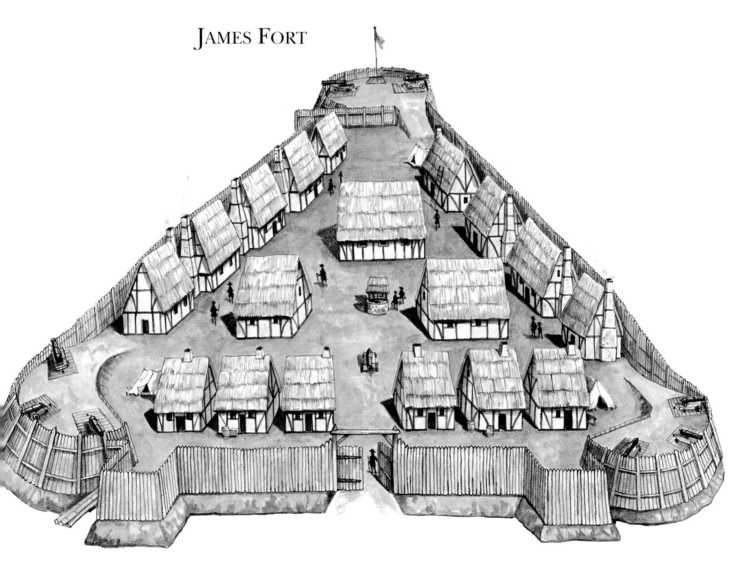

*A colony is a **territory** that is ruled by another country. Jamestown was ruled by England. The Jamestown **colonists** worked hard to clear the land and build homes. They were often sick or hungry, but they did not leave. They stayed and made Jamestown their home.*

is for **kitchen**. The kitchen was the main room in many colonial homes. Girls and women baked bread, churned butter, and cooked meals there. It had a huge fireplace and was very hot in summer. Some families had their kitchen in a small building apart from the main house.

*1. Dog power turned meat over the fire. A **spit** was attached to the dog's wheel. When the dog ran, it turned the wheel and the spit. 2. To keep them from going bad, apples and herbs were hung to dry. 3. Bread was baked in a bread oven over a smaller fireplace.*

is for **leather worker**. Leather workers made goods from animal hides. One kind of leather worker was the saddle and harness maker. He was very busy because colonists traveled on horseback or in wagons and coaches. They often needed new saddles, harnesses, and saddlebags.

This leather worker is making a portmanteau. *Portmanteau means "coat carrier" in French. This small suitcase held a coat and other clothes. The clothes were rolled instead of folded for packing. Try rolling your clothes when you pack for a trip. You can pack much more!*

is for **milliner**. Milliners mended clothes and sewed simple dresses. They sold gloves, feathers, buttons, and lace, as well as fancy gowns that were made in Europe. The hats shown below also could be found at the milliner's shop. In colonial times, almost everyone wore a hat.

(above) A mobcap was an everyday hat.

This milliner is measuring cloth for a hooded cloak. The two large hats on the right were popular near the end of the 1700s.

is for **neckwear**. Neckwear covers the neck and upper chest. Scarves and ties are neckwear. Neckwear was popular with both men and women. It looked good and kept a person's neck warm. Women also used it to cover their chest because many dresses were low cut.

solitaire

cravat

stock

modesty piece

choker

nosegay

*Several kinds of neckwear are shown above. Some people also wore **nosegays**, or flowers, near their nose to keep from smelling the body odors of other people. People did not bathe often!*

17

is for **outbuildings**. People who owned farms or large homes often had outbuildings behind their main house. Kitchens, barns, smoke houses, chicken coops, and spring houses were some outbuildings. The toilet was also in a separate building. It was called a **necessary**.

*The **corn crib** kept corn from going moldy. Its legs kept the corn away from mice.*

*Chickens lived in **chicken coops**. They laid their eggs on straw.*

Meat and fish were smoked in the **smoke house** *to keep them from going bad.*

*A **spring house** was built over a spring. Milk was stored in the cold water.*

 is for **plantation**. Plantations were large farms where one main crop was grown to be sold for money. There were cotton, tobacco, and rice plantations. They were owned by wealthy **masters**, but **slaves** did most of the work. Slaves were people who were forced to work without pay.

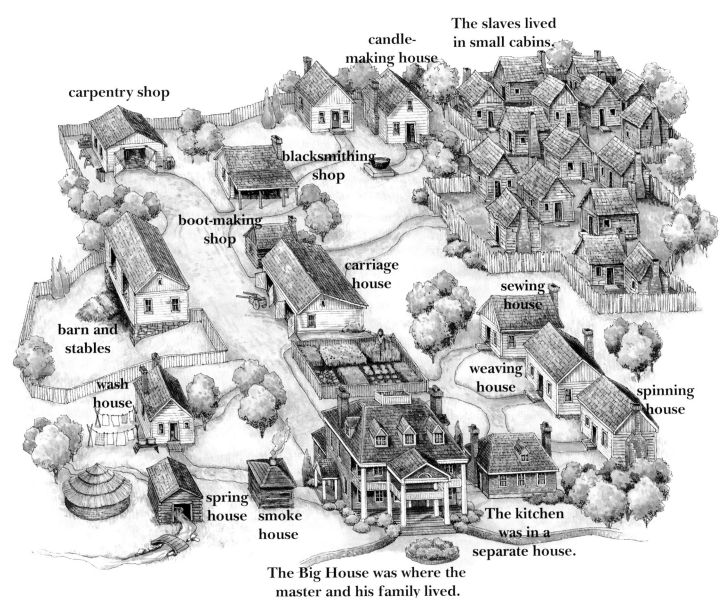

candle-making house

The slaves lived in small cabins.

carpentry shop

blacksmithing shop

boot-making shop

carriage house

sewing house

weaving house

spinning house

barn and stables

wash house

spring house

smoke house

The kitchen was in a separate house.

The Big House was where the master and his family lived.

Almost everything that was needed by the master, his family, and his slaves was made on the plantation. Some slaves worked in the different workshops. A few worked as cooks or servants in the Big House. Most of the slaves, however, worked in the fields.

is for **quoits**. Quoits was a popular game among colonial children. It was played by tossing a rope or metal ring onto a stake called a **hob**. Colonial children also enjoyed flying kites, playing with marbles, walking on stilts, and rolling a hoop with a stick.

is for **reel**. A reel is a yarn winder. After the colonists spun wool into yarn, they wound it onto a reel to keep it from tangling. The reel turned and measured the yarn as it was wound. Each 40 turns made one **skein** of yarn. The skeins were used for weaving and knitting.

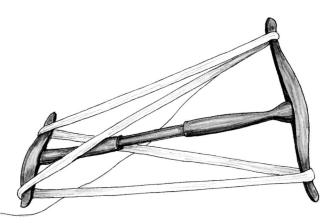

*A **niddy noddy** is a simple reel. Yarn was wound by hand around the reel.*

*A **clock reel** counted the number of turns. At forty turns, it made a loud snapping noise to signal that a skein was finished.*

skein of yarn

is for **stocks**. When people were found guilty of not paying their bills or stealing, they had to spend time in the stocks. Their ankles were locked in so that they could not pull out their feet. People walked by and made fun of the prisoners. Some even threw garbage at them.

Spending time in the stocks was very embarrassing!

JAMES CRAIG

① ② ③ ④ ⑤

S is also for **signs**. Signs advertised shops, workshops, and taverns. Many colonists could not read, so signs had pictures as well as words. Look at the signs on these two pages. Match them to the businesses listed here. The answers are in the box below.

A. boot maker
B. apothecary
    (there are two signs)
C. gunsmith
D. silversmith

E. milliner
F. tavern
G. grocer
H. cabinet maker
I. wig maker

(6)

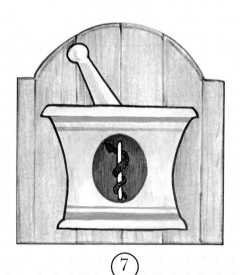

(7)

(8)

(9)

(10)

Answers

A-9; B-7 & 10; C-3; D-2; E-8; F-5; G-1; H-6; I-4

The **mortar and pestle** (7) and the rhinoceros (10) were both symbols of the apothecary. The mortar and pestle were used to grind and store medicines. People believed that rhinoceros horns had the power to heal. A silversmith advertised his shop using a golden ball (2), even though he did little work with gold. He thought the golden ball made him seem more important because gold is worth more than silver.

T is for **trades**. Trades were jobs done by people with special skills. Tradespeople made things such as clothes, horseshoes, and saddles. Look at the objects on these two pages. Match them to the tradespeople in the list below. The answers are at the bottom of the next page.

A. printer
B. housewright
C. miller
D. leather worker
E. founder

F. blacksmith
G. tailor
H. cabinet maker
I. wheelwright
J. cooper

①

②

③

④

5

6

7

Clues: Number 8 is an **inkball**. The cooper made one of the things mentioned on page 11. For more information on the founder, see the letter Z (page 31).

8

10

9

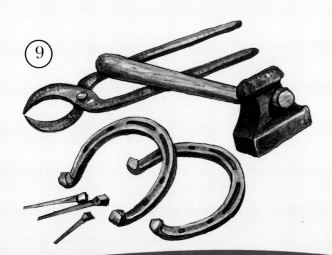

is for **undergarments**. Garment is another word for clothing. Undergarments are underwear. In colonial times, people did not wear underpants. Men and boys wore long shirts that they tucked into their breeches. Girls and women wore a shift next to their skin.

*Girls and women wore their **shift**, a loose cotton or linen dress, all day and night. Stockings were worn by both men and women.*

*Girls and women wore at least two **petticoats** over their shift and under their skirt.*

*A **stay** was worn under a woman's bodice. It was laced tightly to make her waist look small.*

Pockets were sewn onto a belt and worn under the skirt. To reach the pockets, slits were cut into the skirt.

Men's shirts were long enough to cover their backside. They doubled as underwear.

is for **vegetable garden**. Almost everyone had a vegetable garden beside their house. People grew cabbages, tomatoes, beans, and other foods. They ate some of them in summer and autumn and saved the rest for winter. They stored the vegetables in the pantry and cellar.

Many kinds of vegetables were preserved for the winter months. Tomatoes were made into sauce, cucumbers were pickled, cabbages became sauerkraut, and beans and corn were dried. Beets and asparagus were cooked and then sealed in jars.

 is for **wig maker**. A wig maker made, styled, and cleaned wigs. Wig makers were also called **perukers**. Wigs were gray, brown, or white. They were made from human hair, horsehair, or goat hair. Most men wore wigs. Some women also wore wigs, but many styled their own hair.

Huge wigs such as this one were held together with wire.

These two styles were popular in the early 1700s.

This wig was called a bob wig.

The tête de mouton wig had tight curls. The name means "head of a sheep" in French.

The cadogan wig had a looped **queue**. A queue is the tail of the wig.

The hedgehog wig had a fuzzy top.

The bag wig hid its queue inside a bag.

The Ramillies wig had a braided queue.

29

is for **Xmas**. Xmas was the Christian way of writing Christmas. The X stood for the cross, a symbol of the Christian religion. Many colonists worked on Christmas Day. Some went to church and had a special dinner with family and friends. Xmas was not a big holiday until the nineteenth century.

At Christmastime, some masters gave their slaves clothing, cakes, and time off work. House slaves cooked and served the Christmas meal.

is for **your colonial alphabet book**. Your alphabet book could be about different subjects or just one subject such as the kitchen, trades, or clothing. You can also make a picture dictionary. Draw small pictures and name several objects starting with the same letter. Be creative!

Z is for **zinc**. Zinc was a very important metal in colonial times. It was **alloyed** with another metal, called copper, to make brass. A **founder** made many useful brass objects, including candlesticks, keys, bells, shoe buckles, and handles for opening dresser drawers.

Glossary

alloy To melt metals together to create a new metal

apprentice Someone who works for a tradesperson to learn a trade

boarding school A school where students live as they study

cape A sleeveless coat that hangs from the shoulders and is fastened at the neck

cellar A room under a building, used to store food and keep it cold

choker A necklace that fits tightly around the neck

Christian A person who follows the teachings of Jesus Christ

colonial In America, describing the period between the early 1600s and 1776; describing a person or thing that belongs to a colony

colonist A person who lives in a colony

colony A land or place settled and ruled by people of another country

cooper A person who makes barrels

founder A person who uses molds to make metal objects

grocer Someone who owns a food store

herb A plant, such as parsley, used to make medicine or to flavor food

housewright A tradesperson who builds and repairs houses

inkball A leather-covered ball that was used to spread ink on type for printing

Jamestown Founded in 1607, the first permanent English settlement in North America and the first capital of Virginia

linen Cloth made from the fiber of the flax plant

miller A person who operates a mill

modesty piece A ruffle that was attached to a woman's dress to cover her chest

pantry A room near the kitchen for storing dishes and food

spit A metal pole on which meat was turned and roasted over a fire

territory An area of land ruled by a state, nation, or king or queen

water wheel A wheel turned by flowing water and used to power a mill

wheelwright A tradesperson who makes and repairs wheels

Index

activities 23, 24-25, 31
apothecary 4, 23
apprentice 4
boot maker 5, 19, 23
children 6, 7, 8, 9, 11, 14, 20, 26
Christmas *see* Xmas
clothing 5, 6-7, 11, 15, 16, 17, 24, 26, 30, 31
colony 13
dresses 7, 11, 16, 17, 26
education 8
fire 9, 14

fireplace 9, 14
food 9, 10, 12, 14, 18, 19, 27, 30
founder 24, 25, 31
games 11, 20
gristmill 10
hats 6, 16
home 8, 9, 12, 13, 14, 18, 19, 27
hoops 11, 20
horses 5, 15
inn 12
Jamestown 13
kitchen 14, 18, 19, 31

leather worker 5, 15, 24
medicine 4, 23
milliner 16, 23
neckwear 17
outbuildings 14, 18, 19
plantation 19
quoits 20
reel 21
saddle and harness maker 15
shops 4, 5, 16, 19, 23
signs 22-23

slaves 19, 30
stocks 22
tavern 12, 23
toys 11, 20
trades 10, 15, 19, 23, 24-25, 28, 31
undergarments 7, 26
vegetable garden 27
wig maker 23, 28
wigs 28-29
windmill 10
Xmas 30
yarn 21
zinc 31

9 0 Printed in the U.S.A. 6